TO ___Martin and Mari___

FROM ___Trex___

PUBLICATIONS

My Secret Super Power

Copyright © 2017 by ETA Publications. All rights reserved.

All rights reserved. Printed in the United States of America. No part of this book may be used or reproduced in any manner whatsoever without written permission except in the case of brief quotations embodied in critical articles or reviews.

For information contact ETInspires.com

Written by Carlas Quinney

Illustrations by Shiela Alejandro

Book Layout by Kantis Simmons

This book is dedicated to you.

May you forever embrace your superpower.

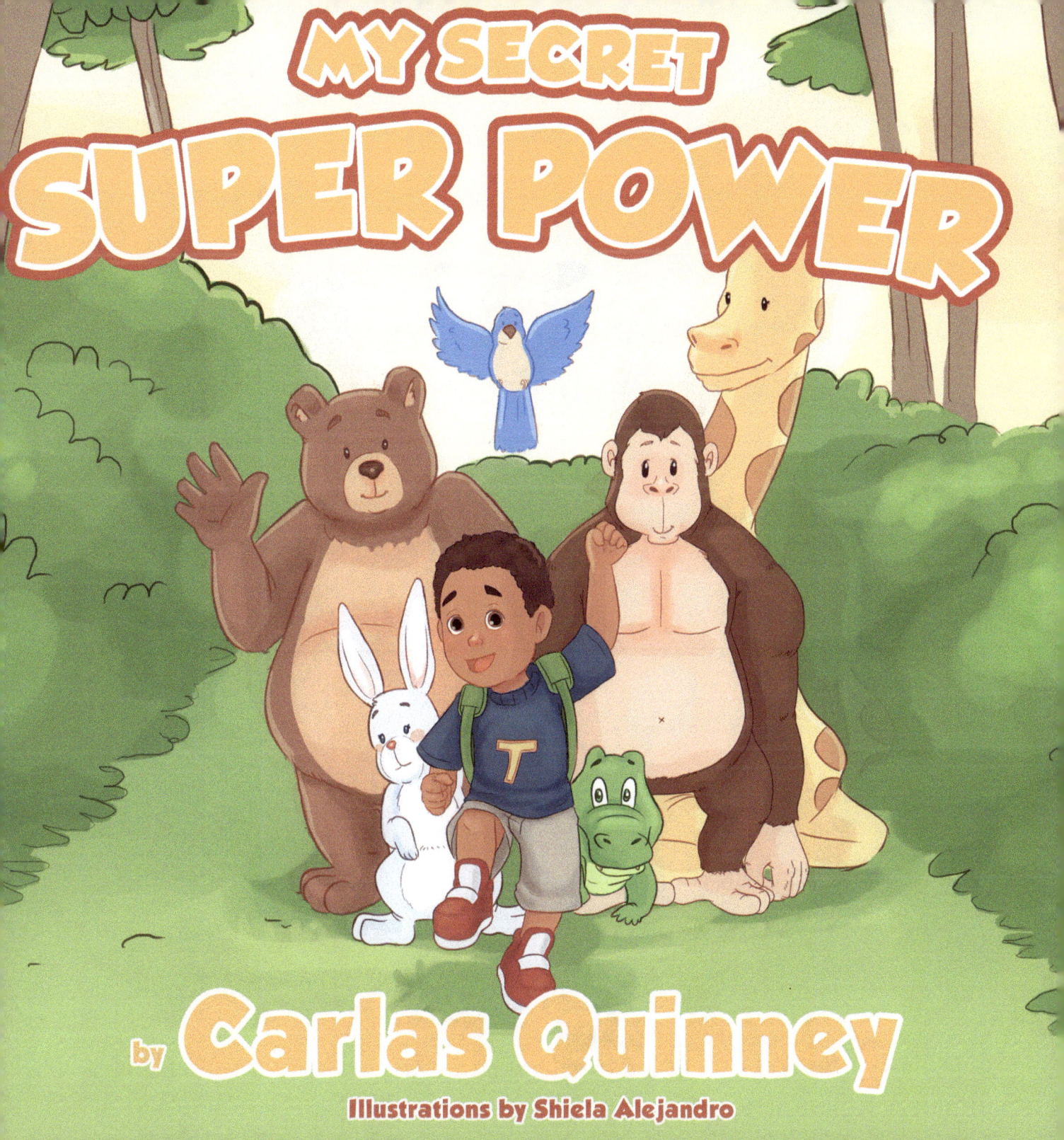

"Daddy, did I tell you about my adventure in the jungle?" asked Trey.

"No, Trey. I do not remember you telling me about your adventure in the jungle," said Daddy.

"Do you want to hear it?"

"Of course I do!" said Daddy.

"OK! One day, on my way home from school, I got lost in a big jungle. Out of nowhere, a little bunny rabbit hopped out from behind a tree . . ."

"Excuse me, Ms. Bunny Rabbit. My name is Trey and I am lost in this big jungle. Do you think you can help me find my house?"

"You can call me Riley," said the rabbit.

"And no! I cannot help you find your house. I am far too small, and I have never even been out of the jungle!"

"Don't worry, Riley. Everybody has a superpower! I bet you can jump really high! Can you jump up and see if my house is behind these tall bushes?"

"You're right, Trey. I CAN jump very high!"

And she began hopping above the bushes, high into the sky.

"I did not find your house, Trey," said Riley, "but I did find Gary the gorilla. Maybe he can help."

"Good afternoon, Gary! Do you think you can help me find my house?"

"No," said Gary, "I cannot help you find your house. I am much too big and way too slow."

"Don't worry, Gary. Everybody has a superpower, and you are very strong," said Trey. "Can you use your strength to knock over these bushes that are blocking our path?"

"I know I can Trey! I AM very strong!" said Gary, and he began knocking over all the bushes that were in their way.

So Trey, Riley, and Gary continued their journey through the jungle looking for Trey's house. All of a sudden they came upon a big river.

"Oh no!" said Trey. "How are we going to get across this big river?"

"What are you guys doing in my river?" said a loud voice.

"YIKES! It's a scary monster!" screamed Riley, "Awww, he's not scary," said Gary. "That's Cody the crocodile."

"Hi, Cody!" said Trey. "I got lost in the jungle on my way home from school. Do you think you can help me find my house?"

"I cannot help you find your house. My arms are much too short and I cannot see very well," said Cody.

"Don't worry, Cody! Everybody has a superpower, and you're an awesome swimmer! Can we ride on your back across the river?"

"You're right," said Cody. "I AM a great swimmer! Everybody hop on and hold on tight!"

So Trey, Riley, and Gary all hopped on Cody's back and rode him to the other side of the river, where they continued their journey through the jungle.

Boom! Boom! Boom! "What are those loud footsteps?" said Trey.

"I don't know, but it doesn't sound good," said Gary.

"Who goes there?" said a loud voice from behind a tree.

"Wait! That sounds like Benny the bear," said Cody.

"Why yes, it is!" said Benny.

"Hi Benny! My name is Trey and I am lost in this big jungle. Can you help me find my house?"

"No, Trey. I cannot help you find your house. I am afraid I'm just too clumsy," said Benny.

"Don't worry Benny, everybody has a superpower! And you can smell really well. We're getting hungry from all this walking. Can you help us find some food?"

"No problem! When it comes to finding food, I AM the best," said Benny. "Right this way" And off they went through the jungle to look for food.

"You did it Benny! I see some food. We can have a picnic!" said Trey.

So Trey, Riley, Gary, Cody, and Benny all sat down and ate their lunch. Just as everyone was taking their last bite, a voice came from way up high.

"Hey, what's going on down there?" said the voice.

"Hey, it's Gini the giraffe!" said Benny.

"Hi Gini! My name is Trey and I got lost in this jungle on my way home from school. It's getting late and I need to get home soon.

Do you think you can you help me find my house?"

"No, I'm afraid I cannot help you find your house, Trey," said Gini. "I am too tall and my head always gets stuck in the trees when I walk."

"Don't worry, Gini," said Trey. "Everybody has a superpower! And because you're so tall you can see really high and far! Do you think you could look over the trees and find my house?"

"You're right, Trey!" said Gini. "I AM very tall and I CAN see very far! Everyone, follow me!"

And off they went looking for Trey's house.

"Do you see my house yet, Gini?" asked Trey.

"No, I don't see your house yet," said Gini.

"But I do see Bella, the bluebird."

"Hi, Bella!" said Trey. "I got lost in the jungle on my way home from school. If I don't get home soon, my daddy is going to start to worry. Can you please help me find my house?"

"No Trey. I'm afraid I cannot help you find your house. My legs are much too short and I will only hold you back."

"Don't worry, Bella," said Trey. "Everybody has a superpower! You have great eyes and can see very far. You have strong wings so you can fly high in the sky.

"Can you fly above the trees and tell me if you can see my house?"

"You're right, Trey! I DO have great eyes and I CAN fly high, give me one second," said Bella.

And off Bella flew, high above the trees.

"Oh wow! I see a big, brown house," said Bella.

"Trey, do you have a big, brown house?"

"Yes, I do! I do have a big, brown house!" said Trey.

"I found it! I found it! Follow me!" said Bella.

And all the friends followed Bella and cheered,

"HOORAY! WE FOUND TREY'S HOUSE!"

Trey thanked his new friends for all their help.

 "We couldn't have done it without you, Riley. If you hadn't jump so high over the bushes, we would have never found Gary. And we couldn't have done it without you, Gary. If you didn't knock over all those bushes, we would have never found Cody at the river.

"We couldn't have done it without you, Cody. If you didn't help us get across the river, we would have never met Benny. We couldn't have done it without you, Benny! If you didn't help us find food, we would have never met Gini.

"And we couldn't have done it without you, Gini. If you weren't so tall, we would have never met Bella. We couldn't have done it without you, Bella. With your great eyes and strong wings, you flew high in the sky and found my house!"

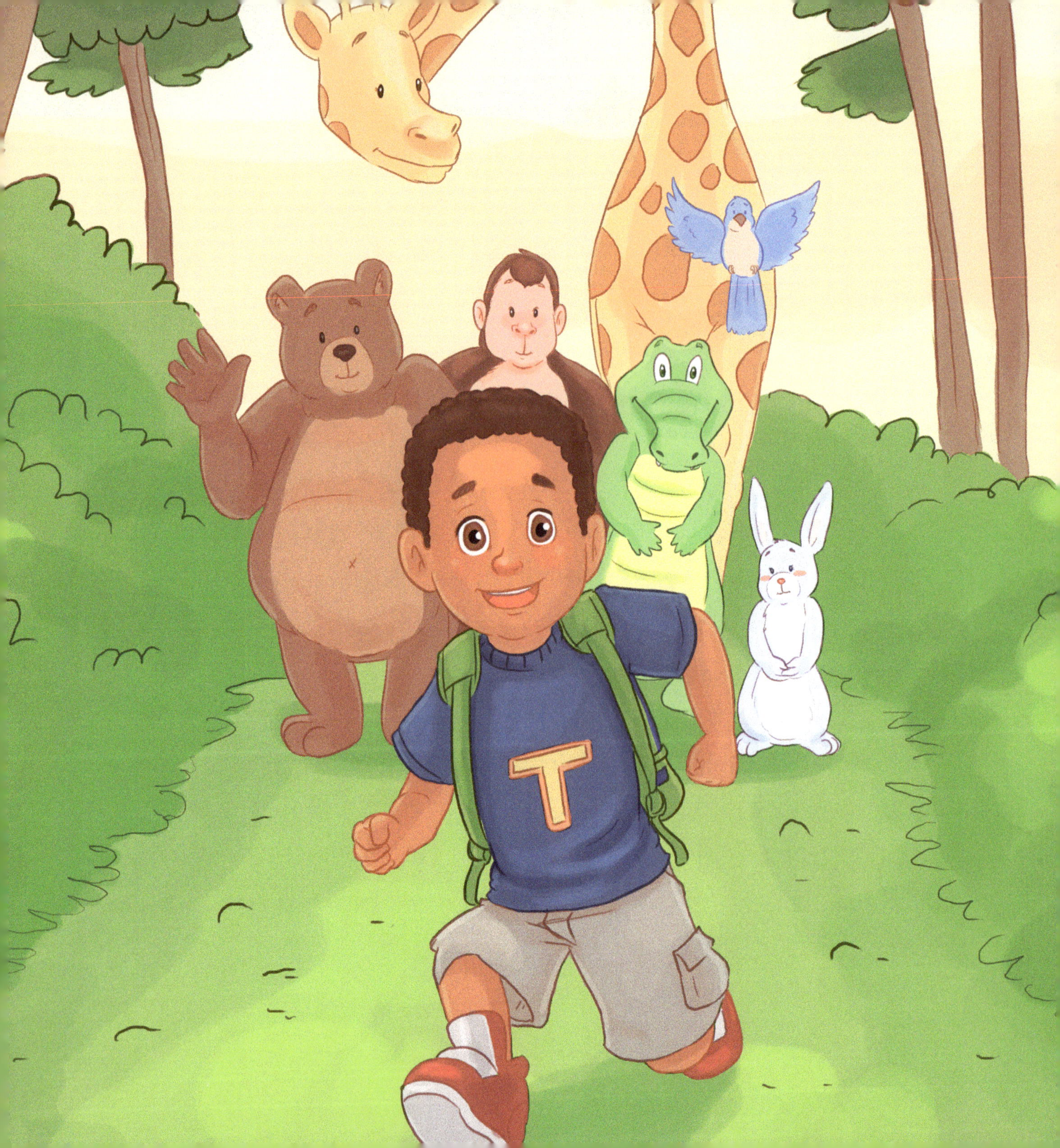

"You all are so awesome!" said Trey.

"Remember to never doubt yourself. We all have our own superpower and we must never be afraid to use it. I have to get going now," said Trey.

"My daddy is waiting on me for dinner. I'll see you all next time."

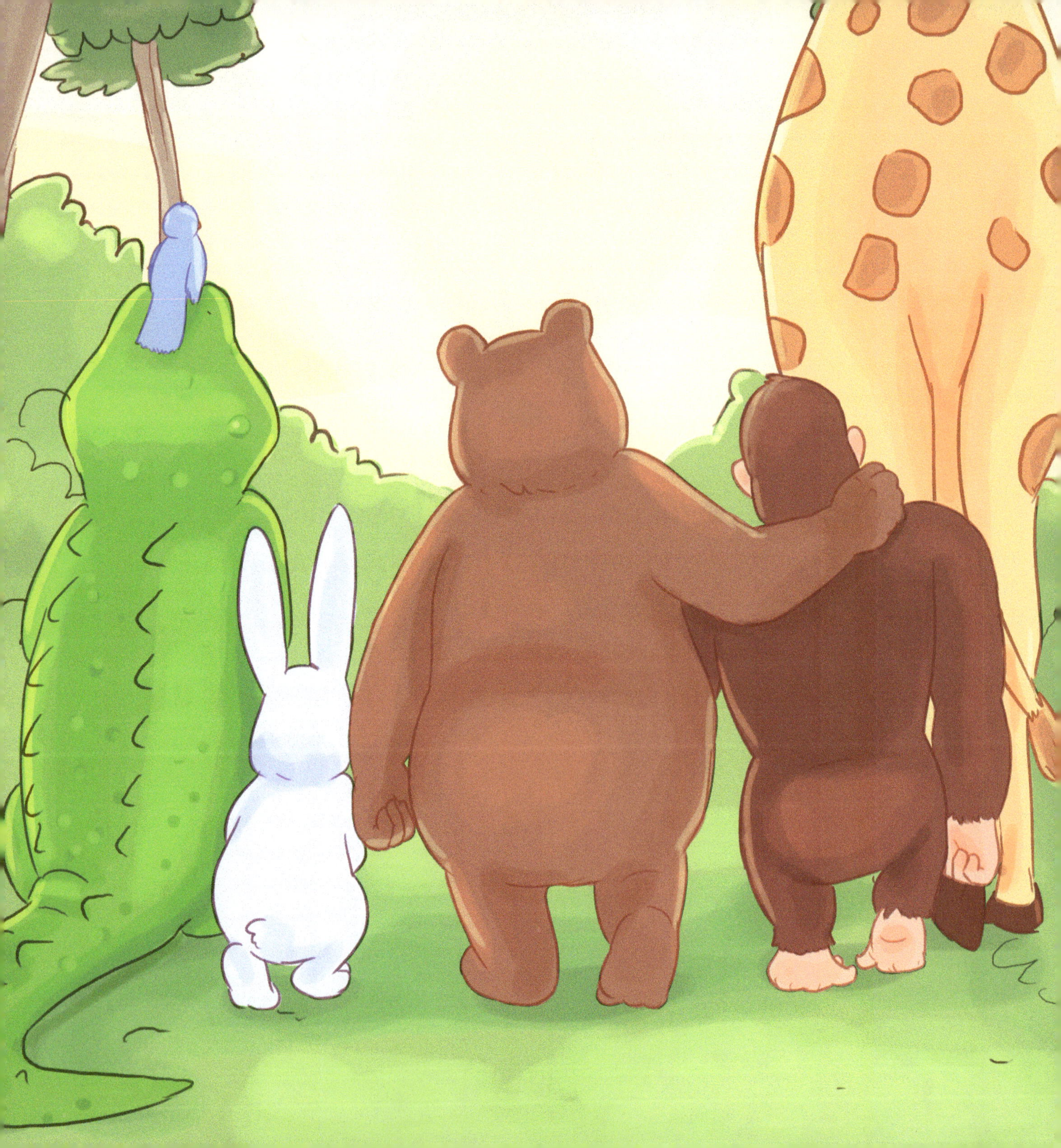

"Bye, Trey," said all of his new found friends as they turned and headed back to their homes.

Trey waved back yelling "Bye friends!", as he ran up the stairs and into his house.

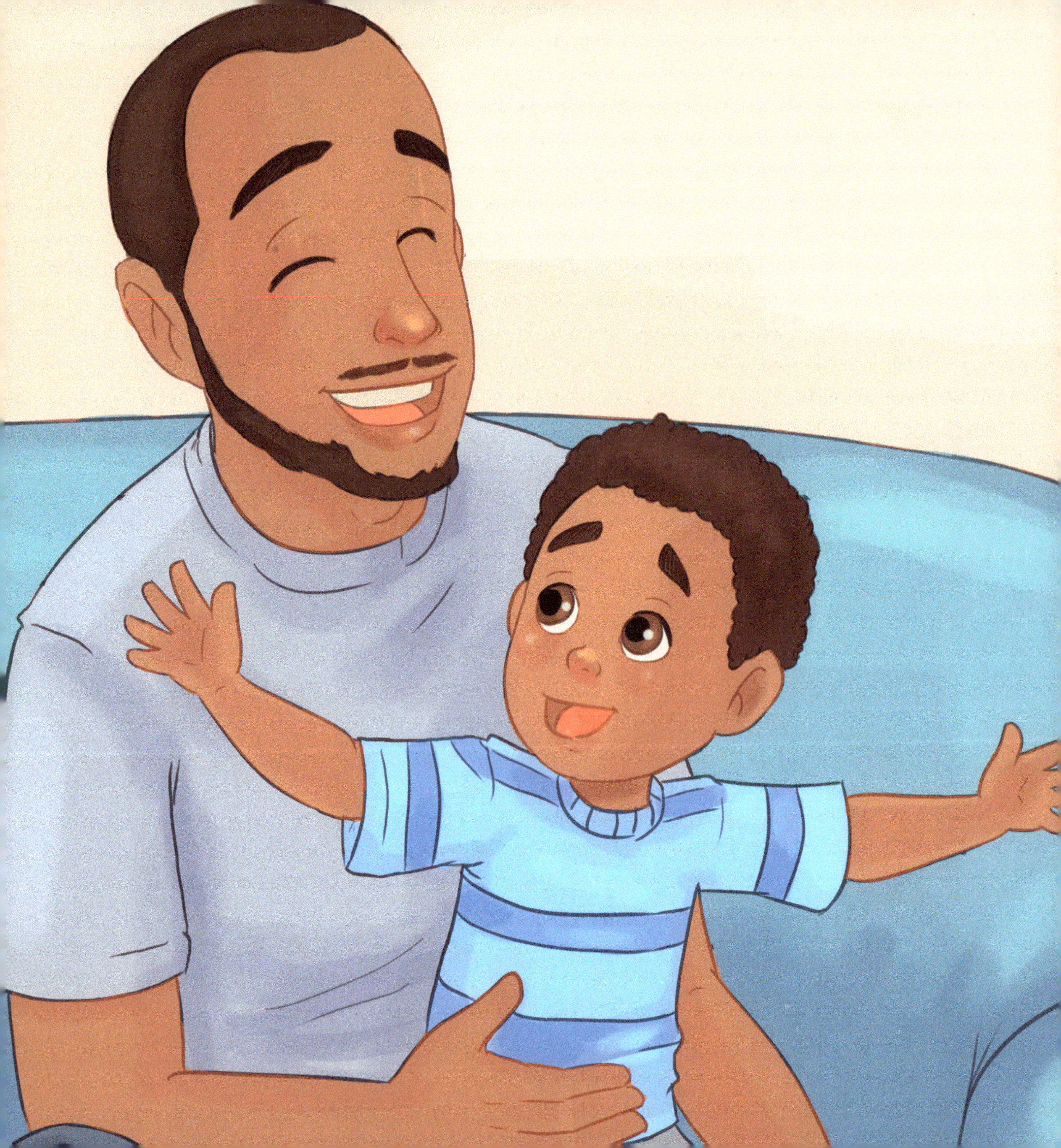

"Trey, that was an amazing story!" said Daddy.

"It's not a story Daddy. That really happened!"

"I believe you. But one last thing, Trey. You never told me what your superpower was."

"Daddy, didn't you figure it out? My superpower is making a lot of really cool friends!"

"And what a great superpower that is to have son! Now, come over here and use your other superpower to help me set the table 'Super Trey!'"

"You got it, Daddy!"

The End

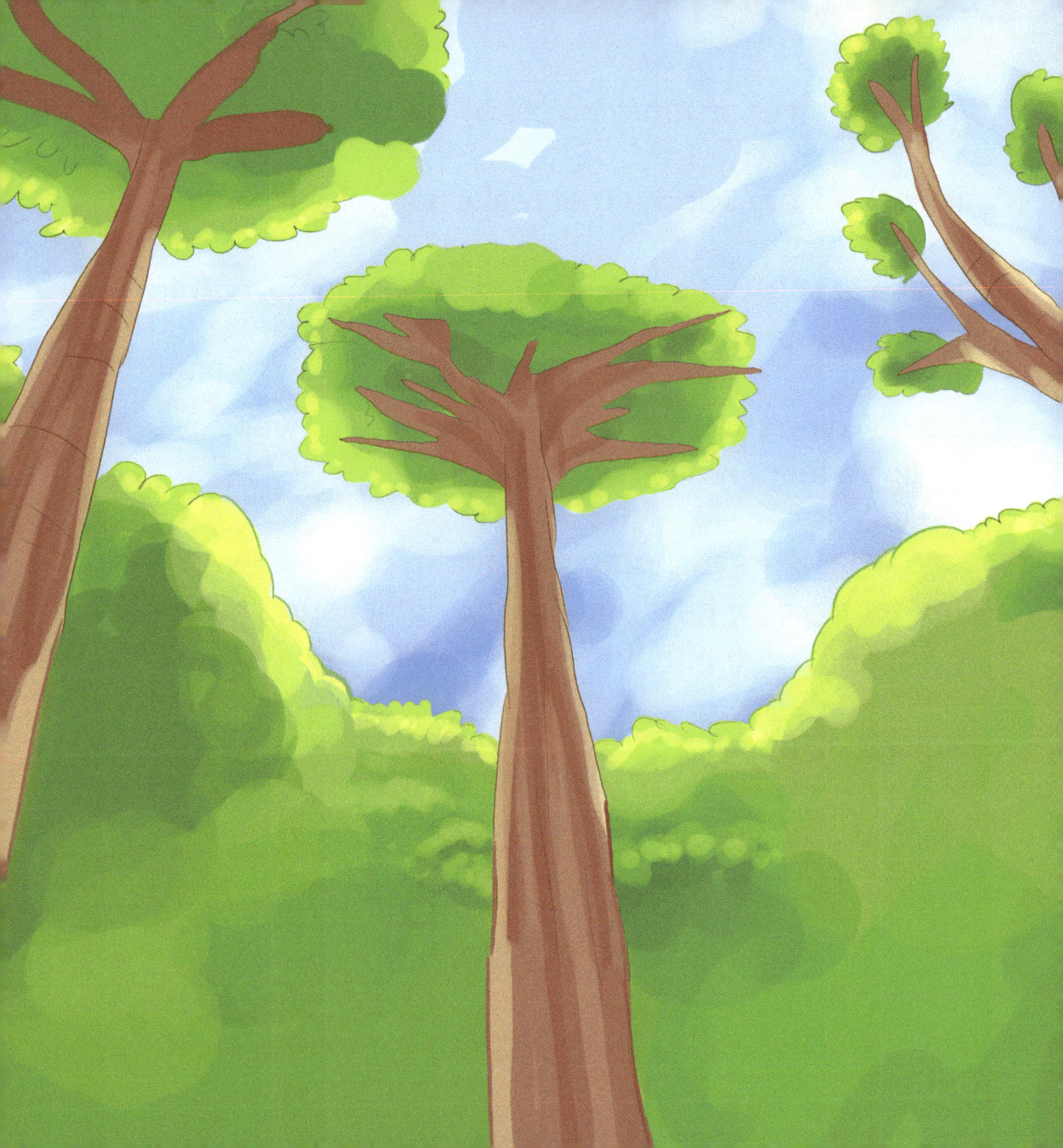

MY NAME IS

_____

MY SECRET SUPER POWER IS

_____

Thank you for taking this adventure with us.

-The Quinneys